create.addanots.start

ANOTS

The Best Way To Deal With Logic.

ANOTS Can Save Your Life.

David Gomadza

www.twofuture.world

PAPERBACK ISBN: 9798338299388

DEDICATION

Signed David Gomadza
www.twofuture.world
04September 2024
16:00pm
Visit www.twofuture.world

TABLE OF CONTENTS

create.addanots.start ANOTS

ACKNOWLEDGMENTS

Tomorrow's World Order

Create.addanotsdavidgomadza.start

[create.addanotsyournamesurname.start

Anots is the most advanced logic situation resolving concept developed by david gomadza that say if there I another option to deal with all situation then anots is the other option david gomadza working on Yahweh's instructed cases where the police and the hospitals target orphans and steal their houses now if we look at the cases most of them is when the orphan died in a humiliating way and as david gomadza analysed the cases he realized that there was more to it than meet the eye the orphans were easily killed for the police it was a matter of saying some scary words and the orphan freezes and once that is so then the police would easily kill him this is exactly what happened because if this was not so then the police would add other tactics to kill the orphan david gomadza witnessed worldwide the police competing to be the best at all levels in the ability to kill fast actually challenging Yahweh the creator and going full blast to kill orphans breaking records now if we look at exactly what happened then this is the case orphans died easily because the police overrided the actual settings and introduced their own terms on all orphans and hence could easily tell when the orphan is likely to die if hit for example in the head if we look at all these cases then we can see a pattern emerging that all the deaths can be attributed to a slow pace in reasoning not because those involved were dull no but because the police changed the settings so that the orphans would die easily by switching between reality and normal this is because in reality no actual death occurs that means the orphan would be thinking that the police man is just checking if they can know when is danger likely to occur but this time actually kill him or not if we ask what can be of the police and the orphans then this is the truth the police work to kill the orphans because the orphans are easy targets and most work to extreme to get out of poverty hence must always be at the top of things that means rich in millions for the most who died in property and housing development now if we ask why most died this is the basic answer they all died because   there was no one who could tell then what was happening in confined situations this is now the known facts

1.   In confined situations our bodies as humans are designed to ignore danger as long as logic is not defined Yahweh the creator had a problem of adjusting the parameters so that height can be included as well as safety you can see that it is difficult for humans to act the same way on heights and on ground level if we ask what happens at heights then this is the answer at heights there is logic at play as well as gravity that means what can be easily achieved at ground level might not be achieved at ground but could not be achieved at heights if we ask what can be of logic and heights then this the answer at height logic is not defined if defined it ignores gravity that means you can put the same logic for the ground level and for the up height level that means the creator the greatest as per david gomadza used height to ignore logic because if he had not done so people would literally jump off buildings to their deaths now if we ask what can be logic in this case then logic is the thing that defines routes if the routes is defined then logic is defined and a person in that situation would escape any confinement situation so if we ask what can be of logic that can't be of height then this is the answer logic cant be defined in terms of height but in terms of defined escape routes if we ask what can be logic then this is the answer logic can be the

only solution to all the orphans murders hence he tried to work out a way to find what can be logic without wasting time the other solution would be to start from the basics and write the correct logic all one by one and this would mean distrusting the creator but what he did is to use exactly what is there and define further what is logic for specific situations and his team of clones his clones came up with the solution they spent hours practicing after being asked what can be logic and what cant be logic and after carefully checking these questions they realized that there is no defined logic for dangerous situation in the manuals of humans hence when it comes to that humans can't know exactly what to do but if we put two extra rules then these make all of them escape except one that need an extra option that of a window hence throughout this time david gomadza [myself as clone part of anots discovered that if we ask what can be logic in dangerous situation the body literally say I don't know hence if humans cant solve this by themselves who can? The creator an add logic to all humans and define the situation but when humans were created the created had other ideas and never thought that murder would be so pronounced as it is today where police office kill orphans to steal their houses that are worth millions now lets look at what can be of humans without anots

WHAT CAN BE HUMANS WITHOUT ANOTS

Humans without anots can be like a creator without followers this is because the creator can always ask what can be of humans without the creator and find solutions where as humans without a creator will find life hard for them if we ask what is to be done then this is the case we can either ask the creator to deal with these issues or as humans we can always find solution ourselves as humans but what can be humans without a creator but with his representative then this is the case and the answer the creator does not need to worry too much about humans because he know they are in good hands and as things are progressing and heading the right directions because david gomadza is determined to find solution to all the questions raised in the book of creation that was there before Yahweh and has already answered Yahweh's question that no one has managed to answer since the days of creation now if we look at what can be the case with these cases there are always deaths associated with the police who deal with orphans this is because there are more of them who do really bad things for quick easy money most as david gomadza found out they assume the orphans appreciated their roles of raising them up but david also found out that if we ask what can be of these police officers and the orphans then this is the answer most of them assume appreciated contribution towards raising them but if we look at what can be of all this then this is not true because according to 99% percent of them they were orphans because of the police who robbed them of their parents through accidents first mainly car accidents having being pushed into other cars or out of the road literally and as such when they find out its bitter food to swallow that help becomes hate enough to kill so if we ask what can be done then this is the situation we can always avoid craving to raise other people's kids the reason being that its all for the wrong reasons for gains as two people rather than to work for yourself and earn a living if we ask what the police think 99% of them think that they deserve respect from these orphans but this is subjective as the good ones rather would work hard than crave for other kids in order to supplement their incomes the main reason is that they find killing orphans easy because no one would come to check or ask for anything after that meaning an easy way of making money and covering up everything we found out that if we are to keep quiet the police would keep going to kill other humans in the hope that if not caught then they would be rewarded at the end of all this but if we ask what can be of humans that can't be of the creator then this is true

WHAT CAN BE HUMANS THAT CAN'T BE OF THE CREATOR

Humans an always be what they want but if we ask what can be of humans that cant be of the creator then this is the answer the creator can be told what humans want and he can then choose a representative who can work on the case and then ask what can be of humans that cant be of others and why this is the case if we ask what can be humans then this is the answer they can be what they want even if the creator is not directly involved they can ask what can be of humans that cant be of the creators normally creators are humans that want to ask what can be of creators but without humans then if we ask what can be of humans who want to be creators then we can also say david gomadza has eyed the position as well because in his search of answers he found out that the creator can make human stencils available for everyone that means the creator is there to make sure that humans get everything they want and as such the creator keeps the stencil after this is the case as David admitted that the creator still has a lot to dish out that means it's a long wait but in good way as the creator and david are both working to find solutions but if we ask what can be of the creator with no humans then we are looking at zeus who died before even developing the first humans if we ask what can be of humans that cant be of the creator then these humans will always want to try something new if we ask what can be of humans that cant be of the creators then this is the answer if we ask what cant be of the creator that can be of humans then this is the answer if we are to ask we can always ask what can't be the case if we ask what can be of the creator and humans then this is the answer humans will always be humans as the creator will always be the creator and as such humans will always ask the creator to fix things if he cant hence to appoint someone who can humans can always ask the creator for answers and if the answers are there then we can say that the creator can always be there for us if we ask what is to be of people and the creator then this is the answer the creator will always be there and will always be there for humans but if we ask what can be of the creator that cant be of humans then this is the answer humans will always be humans and will always be there for humans now lets ask some serious questions that can be there and can help us define what anots are now lets look at all these cases and decide what to do in normal situations then we compare with what happened

1. If we die who is to blame ourselves
2. If we die who is to blame ourselves
3. If death comes who is to blame ourselves
4. If we die what can be done nothing
5. If we die what can be death death can come again
6. What death is and how death is death by dying
7. What can be death and how anything in life is misused or inappropriately can be death alcohol can be death women can be death
8. What is death and why death is the only way out for those in trouble
9. What can be death and when anytime is death time
10. What can be death and how and why anything anyhow and for no reason
11. What death is dying is death
12. What death was death and still death only thing that does not change
13. What is to be death and why same because death cant change
14. What was death and when still death and time
15. What can be death and when anything anyhow
16. What Is to be death and why anything no reason

17. What was death and when still death and time
18. What was death still death
19. What can be death and if yes then when anything yes anytime
20. What was death and how death was death by dying
21. What has been death death and still death
22. If death then how by dying
23. If not death then what is this nothing is not death everything is
24. What was death and with what still death with dying
25. What can be death and with what anything anything
26. What is death and how dying dying
27. What can be death and when anything anytime
28. What was death and how still death and anyhow
29. What can be death and with what anything anything
30. What was death still death
31. What is death with what still death anything
32. What can be death and when anything anytime
33. What was death and how still death anyhow
34. What can be death and which anything anything
35. What was death and how dying still dying
36. What can be death and if yes when anything yes anytime
37. What was death and what anything anything
38. What can be death and how anything anyhow
39. What is death and with what dying anything
40. What is death and when dying anytime
41. What can be death and how anything anyhow
42. What was death and how and when
43. If what then how dying what
44. What can be death death
45. What was death still death
46. What could be death death
47. What was death death and dying
48. What will be death still death
49. What an be death but how still death anyhow
50. What was death and with what still death anything
51. What was death and when still death anytime
52. What can be death and with what anything anything

53. What was death and when dying anytime
54. What could be death and how anything anyhow
55. What was death and when dying and anytime
56. What can be death and if not now then when anything anytime
57. What was death before all this and with what dying anything
58. If death then how dying
59. If not death then with what dying
60. What can be of death death anytime
61. What was death dying
62. What is to be death still death
63. What can be death death
64. What was death death
65. What was death and with what dying anything
66. What can be death and with what anything anything
67. What is death dying
68. What could be death still dying
69. What was death dying
70. What can be death dying
71. What was death dying
72. What is death dying
73. What could still be death and with what dying anything
74. What was death like before dying
75. What can death still be like dying
76. What was death and with what dying anything
77. What could be death and with what dying warning
78. What was death and with what death
79. What can still be death and when anything anytime
80. If what then what if death and what
81. If what if then what with anything
82. If what if then with what anything
83. What was death dying
84. What could still be death dying
85. What can be death anything
86. What was death with what dying anything
87. What can still be death with what dying
88. What was death dying
89. What can be death dying

90. What could be death dying

91. If death then with what anything

92. What was death before dying

93. What can still be death death

94. What can still be death with what anything

95. What can be death anything

96. What could be death anything

97. What was death dying

98. What can still be death dying

99. What is death dying

100.   What was death dying

101.   What is death dying

102.   What can still be death dying

103.   What if if what

104.   What can be death anything

105.   What is death with anything

106.   What was death with anything

107.   What can still come with death anything

108.   what death is dying

109.   what can be death dying

110.   what was death

111.   what can be death with death

112.   What was death death

113.   What can still be death death

114.   What was death death

115.   What is death death

116.   What can be death death dying

117.   What is death death

118.   What was death death

119.   What is to be death death

120.   what can be death death

121.   what was death death

122.   what is death dying

123.   what could be death dying

124.   what was death dying

125.   what can be death death

126.   what was death dying

127.   what is death dying

128.	what could be death dying
129.	what is death death
130.	what was death like dying
131.	what could still be death death
132.	what is death
133.	what can death feel like
134.	what can be death
135.	what was death
136.	what is death
137.	what was death
138.	what if we ask a lot of question
139.	what is death
140.	What can be death
141.	What could still be death
142.	What can death be with
143.	What was death
144.	What is death
145.	What was death
146.	What is death
147.	What was death
148.	What is death
149.	What if we ask about death
150.	What can be death
151.	What is death
152.	What can be death
153.	What was death like
154.	What can still be death
155.	What could death come with
156.	What is death for all
157.	What is death for some
158.	What can be death
159.	What could be death
160.	What can be death
161.	What was death
162.	What can still be death
163.	What is death with what can death be like
164.	Death with what
165.	Death with who

166.	Death by who
167.	Death if you want by whom
168.	What id death itself
169.	Who guides death
170.	What can be death but is not
171.	What could be death but is not
172.	What can be death but is not
173.	What is death and with what
174.	What can be death but is not
175.	What could be death but how
176.	What is death and with what
177.	What can be death but how
178.	What was death like
179.	What is death like
180.	What can cause death
181.	What can be death
182.	What is death
183.	What can be death and with what
184.	What is death and what can be death without
185.	What is death
186.	What is not death
187.	What can be death but is not
188.	What could be death and how
189.	What can be death but is not
190.	What is death
191.	What can be death
192.	What was death and with what
193.	What can be death but with what
194.	what is death and when
195.	what is to be death
196.	what is not to be death
197.	what can be death
198.	what if death cones
199.	what can bring death
200.	who can bring death
201.	what is death
202.	what was death
203.	what can be death and with what

204. what has been death
205. what could be death
206. what was death
207. what is death
208. what was death
209. what is death
210. what was death
211. what is death and with what
212. what can be death but is not and why
213. what is death and when
214. what can be death and how
215. what was death
216. what is death
217. what can be death
218. what is death and when
219. what can be death but is not
220. what can be death and when
221. what could be death
222. What was death
223. What is death
224. What was death
225. What is and is not death
226. What can be death
227. What could be death
228. What can be death
229. What was death before
230. What was death
231. What was death
232. What is to be death
233. What can death be
234. What is to be death
235. What was death if not death then how
236. What can be death
237. What is death
238. What was death
239. What is to be death
240. What can be death
241. Now we looked at the whole spectrum of death if we

look at every stage we can see that death comes in all kinds of shapes hence the 240 spectrum calibration if it was predefined parameters these would have been around 107 but when it comes to death there are so many things that can bring death death can come at any time and to every man that means that if not prepared death an surprise us but death is not for all people some overcome death but some succumb forever and never to return again

242.   If we ask what we can do with these questions we can answer all fast as we can see so now we can go to the questions and answer just next to the questions and fast

We can now look at death as if it never happened because if death had happened then some of the answers would have been different so death has never occurred and can't occur for a very long foreseeable future but if we ask what can be of death then this is the answer death can be of many shapes and sizes hence we must look closely to how that can be

DEATH WITH CONFINEMENT

Death is the result of being trapped in a room with the killer as we found out in our research a list of books will be at the end now if we look at what can be of humans that cant be of others now lets look at all cases and the main issues with confinement then we can resolve all these issues easily as pointed out by david gomadza in all his recent books as we started to read easily by embedding the books and reading then fast and understanding them better and you can ask for them [to be action potentials] then if we ask what can be then this is the answer we can always ask what can be of everyone else who ask about what can be done we can always ask what is to be and with what and this is the answer with anots if we look at all the cases david gomadza solved all issues with anots as anots clearly defined what is needed and how to deal with the situation now if we ask what can be done if there is nothing that can be done them we can always as for help but we created a simple way to deal with these situations like adding anots to oneself first through a simple create code

create.addanotsyournameandsurname.startx8.initialise.now.start Now this needs initializing because it has your name already unless if already there meaning just reboot it now we can see that if we ask what can be done then this is the answer we can always go back and check all cases one by one and see what can be done for that case in the case of Revelle Balmain-smith we can see that she could simply not run because logic was not defined logic was not there as escape routes where literally deleted from her system and as it turns out no one even us had escape routes these were deleted by zues because waaaaaer stole by drawings and I was upset and deleted all escape routes since they were mine I wrote the rules and he said I can amend yours only but for nothing or death so I deleted them] zues who said I will but keep an eye on you for a while because all you are doing waaaaaer is to delete all my name only and keep everything then we humans suffered as these routes were not there but now as the representative of the creator we have established an easy way to deal with the situation if we ask what can be done then this is the answer we can always define what are escape routes but

these can still create the same problem as before of dealing with heights and people above sea level so we sat down and discussed all this and came up with an easy solution that means that if we can ask what are anots anots are easy ways of identify escape routes they act as the best way out of a situation if we ask what can be done then this is the case we can always be there to decide what is right and make our own decisions as to the correct way to escape death now lets ask them one by one what can be done with anots
1 laura Vaughan she said I escaped because the road was clearly defined
2. Elle Estelle-parkinson escaped the only one to escape
3. Revelle Balmain-smith I escaped but only as he had grabbed my arm but I managed to escape as he froze
4. Rob adel I escaped but may be the water might still kill me
These are just a few cases we mention for privacy reason but as you can see clearly now what was missing was logic when sitting down if escape routes are missing logic is not defined and all humans because if a person is sat down facing the wall the body will not stand up because logic says you can run through the wall but if you define logic as that every wall is a door then the body will run to the wall and then is further defined that then find escape routes the body can simple then run straight to the door and escape and where the door is locked and a window is provided the body can run to the window and escape by breaking the window that can freeze the killer further but I want to stress out that there might be more to it as other things could have got the orphans easily killed we are looking at another further explanation to do with Australian atm USA asm Canadian aty Scottish assm[arst] british stupid etc which were put at birth most to kill the orphans but then as they become rich the mission changed to protecting them but then now the greedy police officers changed these settings and now mirror-imaged the rich orphans so that they become the lever ones as their password anode and asat are at the bottom meaning in these orphans these three become placed at the top hence if the slow reactions to the problem if but not because they are not clever the reason why they

made millions is because they are clever hence the attention so its to do with this arrangement that if the police are there they can whisper words that cause them to do things they would not otherwise do as a mirror image the words are absorbed by the mirror image the orphans and processed much faster instantly that cause them to freeze but I will write another book to detail all this after looking at more cases but in the mean time you can read this book Earth2 so in short

but I think its only humans that have been tampered with the police as they might have reversed the creator's settings of putting password anode and asat at the bottom in humans instead of at the top I have discovered that the police might have mirror imaged the orphans reversing what the hospitals did at birth hence now the password anode and asat became at the top of Yahweh's

4 THE FINAL CONCLUSION

Extracted from Earth2 by David Gomadza

WHAT IS ANOTS

Anots is the safest system ever designed by a god or a human being for anots makes all situations clear to deal with without engaging with danger if I ask right now what is anots this is the answer anots is a safe system of processes designed to protect human these are but not in priority

1. Advanced awareness this entails advanced warning systems that dictate danger from a radius of 500 meters to 8 seconds these tell humans how to deal with each and every solution so here is the list
    1. aware= raise your head all the time then look left first middle then right

2. unsure = raise your head constantly frequently and check left or right depending with situation

3. arose = raise you head and run first steps then stop

4. arise =raise your head and run first for 28 seconds then stop and check then think about the situation

5. atore = raise your head up high ask what can be done with the situation then sprint the fastest then check the answer this enables the brain to think faster as well

6. attire = raise the head and skid front then run the fastest

7. attire = raise the head and jog first then sprint then stop ask what can be done then sprint again for good

8. attirest = raise the head and ask what was is and likely to be of this situation then sprint fast

9. attirestot = raise the head sprint first then stop ask what was is and likely to be of this situation then sprint for 28 seconds stop only to hear the answer then sprint fast away now if we check you will see that all apply to all dangerous situations and must be obeyed but in any order now we go deeper anots is designed to ask the killer 80 questions

80 QUESTIONS TO ASK THE KILLER SILENTLY

1. Who are you 33nam
2. What do you do 33doo
3. What can be of you today 33tod
4. What was of you yesterday 33yes
5. What do you want 33wan
6. What is of you forever 33youfor
7. What was of you 33was
8. What is likely to happen today 33haptod
9. What is likely to be of us today 33likus
10. Who is to blame 33blam
11. What is likely to happen to me 33hapme
12. What is likely to happen to you 33hapyou
13. What was that you looking for 33look
14. What is that you want 33wan

15. What can be of us both 33bothus
16. What will be of us 33willus
17. What is to be of your conscience 33con
18. What can be of you without me 33youwitme
19. What can be of us together 33ustog
20. Who to blame 33blamwho
21. Who to trust after all this 33truwho
22. Who is likely to die in your opinion
23. Who to cry today 33crywho
24. Who to say I told you 33itolyou
25. Who to speak to after 33speaft
26. Who to run after 33runaft
27. Who can ask why after 33whyaft
28. Who can ask what if after 33whaif
29. Who can say I am in danger 33dan
30. Who can say I was there but I escaped 33there
31. Who are you are 33who
32. Who you want is it me and why 33me?
33. What can be of killers 33kil
34. What was of killers 33kilwas
35. What is to be of killers 33killbe
36. What was that can't be 33wasbut
37. What is but still could be 33isbutstil
38. What could be of killers with vengeance 33ven
39. What might be of killers 33mig
40. What should be of killers 33shokil
41. What could be but is not 33counot
42. What was but is still 33wasbutis
43. What must be but is not 33musbutnot
44. What can be but is not 33canbutnot
45. What must be but can't be 33mustcant
46. What was but is not 33wasbutnot
47. What is but can be 33iscan be
48. What was and could still be 33wascoustibe
49. If I then what 33ifithewha
50. What can be 33wcb

51. What could be 33wcb2
52. What can be 33whacanbe
53. What was is to be 33whatwasis

Anots proposed by davidgomadza by a series of questions that were designed to invoke great answers in order to solve why humans die easily when faced with danger most to an extend that they simply were the answer this is the breakdown of the question

1. What cause humans to do die easily
2. What can be done to prevent easy deaths?
3. What is to blame
4. Who is to blame creator humans or gods
5. Who is to answer calls for help
6. What can be done to change the situation?
7. Who to answer human calls for help God or another human
8. If not humans then who to blame
9. Did the 105 adjustments contribute to human deaths
10. What can be of humans that can't be of gods

Now after looking at all these questions it came clear that a lot of information was missing humans were not create for intelligence purpose because critical system operations were missing how can a creator not design and escape routes if he care about humans in fact escape routes were depreciated meaning deleted forever by ats on 18 afterone $00000^{28}10$ he said I can just make sure that WAAAAAER be blamed for everything if I depreciate all escape routes that way we will become so rich fast but then maybe did to him what he did to zeus to change safe systems by removing the advanced escape routes it's a tit for tart that means safety was either never meant to be but could have been deleted so that if we are to ask what can be of humans without safety escape routes this is the answer safety systems must be adhered to but if we look at all humans apart from [me] davidgomadza no one has safety system if trapped 100% will die this is a design flaw but we cant say that its sabotage only but a business partnership WAAAAAER put ats as judge over the council that approved plans that meant everything was to be as with the others now WAAAAAER removed advanced safety systems to punish zeus so that if the plans are reviewed then the removal of advanced safety systems would make the council object to his plans

 This would give WAAAAAER plans advantage over zeus advanced safety systems but WAAAAAER had a tip off that his own plans had been tampered with as well so he decided to just kill zeus but all this were tricks by business partners zeus strongest area is safety while WAAAAAER strongest is harvest when empty stocks put WAAAAAER if stocks nearly full recall zeus but the huge demand has meant that WAAAAAER remains now let's look at zeus advanced human safety systems zeus wrote that he would propose the most advanced safety system known to humans and drew 18 points of references that will be looked at in line with what he had in mind he said if I am to ask what can be of humans these are the responses I get humans can be what they want but are constrained with so many missing safety precautions what can humans do in face of missing escape routes and safety systems humans can be safe if safety is made a priority that means as the creator its my responsibility to write down what safety precautions for then to adopt in danger

Anots is the only possible logic explanation for every event because with anots everything is clearly defined and your body will respond as if you were already program the cases we looked at as part of David Gomadza team as his clone is to identify what can be done to alleviate the suffering and the number of deaths and this made us come up with anots anots is safe and can be used to find a safe way and safe passage through all this and make escape routes be easily identified meaning the probability of escape having been increased to include that of deciding as well what to do if we look at anots then we can easily say that anots can be and will be used to develop good safe practices of dealing with situations if we ask what can be done then this is the answer we can always hope that if people are trapped in situations that can be dangerous then these people will be able to escape easily given the danger and risk of death now lets look at what can be anots and not because anots is not just a safe system of maneuvering but also of deciding what can be done if we ask this is what can be done we can always ask if we are to go to work and we are trapped on the motorway what can be anots used for or if we are caught up in a hostage situation we can always say we are in a better situation than before if we ask what can be of others who cant escape then this is the fact these people are clever but they just caught up if we ask everyone who died they were the best in terms of thinking and money as some had millions and houses hence were clever hence there must be something going on with all of them if we are to ask one by one most would agree they were the best but and all this is due to the fact that they acted slowly until they were caught up once that had happened then life began looking precariously and were all killed easily for a human being who can fight back all within seconds with the killers breaking records of the easiest kill etc but this will change with anots for anots will guide people and show them that there was an easy way to deal with all these situations now lets look at what can be done in all these situations for anots is there to do what needs doing that is to show the way but how do we decide what can be done if we are to be truthful when we are in the dark the easiest way is to show people what can be done then let them show us their version in this case we are sure to act if we ask what is anots then this is the answer anots is a new way to deal with situations that involve the risk of death do you wait to die or to be killed or you would kill or wait to be killed but if we are to ask what can be done then we can always be at easy with nature and say that we can be ready when time come

The world can be a safe place for everyone for orphans and other people as it might take time to convince others that anots work and that lives can be saved with anots
Once again this is how to add anots to yourself or even your computers or anything simply write create.addanots.start
Currently anots is free but will be commercialized in the future
Visit www.twofuture.world

FURTHER READING

A LIST OF ALL CASES I HAVE LOOKED AT

1. How To Find All Missing Persons. And Collect All Reward Offers. The Formula. Volume II: THE CASE OF TONI TIKI Paperback — May 13, 2024
2. How To Find All Missing Persons / Unsolved Cases. And Collect All Reward Offers. Volume V.: THE CASE OF DANAE WILLIAMS. Paperback — May 17, 2024
3. How To Find All Missing Persons And Collect All Rewards. The Formula. Volume III: THE CASE OF FAWN MARIE MOUNTAIN Paperback — May 16, 2024
4. How To Find All Missing Persons: And Collect All Reward Offers. THE CASE OF MADELEINE McCANN Paperback — May 9, 2024
5. How To Find All Missing Persons / Unsolved Cases. And Collect All Reward Offers. Volume VI: THE CASE OF CHRISTINE MARIE EASTIN Paperback — May 19, 2024
6. How To Find All Missing Persons / Unsolved Cases. And Collect All Reward Offers. Volume VII.: THE CASE OF AMBER ELIZABETH CATES. Paperback — May 19, 2024

7. How To Find All Missing Persons. And Collect All Reward Offers. Volume IV.: THE CASE OF BRIANN MAITLAND. The Most Violent Case In History. Paperback – May 16, 2024

8. How To Find All Missing Persons / Unsolved Cases. And Collect All Reward Offers. Volume VIII: THE CASE OF TAMMY MAHONEY Paperback – May 21, 2024

9. How To Find All Missing Persons / Unsolved Cases. And Collect All Reward Offers. Volume XIII.: THE CASE OF RAELENE MAY EATON. Paperback – May 25, 2024

10. How To Find All Missing Persons / Unsolved Cases. And Collect All Reward Offers. Volume X.: THE CASE OF DEVON SINCLAIR MARSMAN Paperback – May 25, 2024

11. How To Find All Missing Persons / Unsolved Cases. And Collect All Reward Offers. Volume X1.: THE CASE OF ANNE CECILLE ZAPPELLI Paperback – May 26, 2024

12. How To Find All Missing Persons / Unsolved Cases. And Collect All Reward Offers. Volume XII.: THE CASE OF YVONNE KAYE WATERS Paperback – May 25, 2024

13. How To Find All Missing Persons / Unsolved Cases. And Collect All Reward Offers. Volume XIV.: THE CASE OF FELICIA MARIA WILSON Paperback – May 27, 2024

14. How To Find All Missing Persons / Unsolved Cases. And Collect All Reward Offers. Volume XV.: THE CASE OF GWENNETH GRAHAM Paperback – May 27, 2024

15. How To Find All Missing Persons / Unsolved Cases. And Collect All Reward Offers. Volume XVII.: THE CASE OF LAURA KATE MUCKERSIE Paperback – May 30, 2024

16. How To Find All Missing Persons / Unsolved Cases. And Collect All Reward Offers. Volume XX.: THE CASE OF LISA GOVAN Paperback – June 2, 2024

17. THE PRACTICAL GUIDE ON HOW TO SOLVE THE MISSING PERSONS OR UNSOLVED CASES WITH REWARD VALUE OF $1 Million Each.: METHODOLOGY: ALL THE TOOLS YOU NEED. Paperback – June 2, 2024

18. How To Find All Missing Persons / Unsolved Cases. And Collect All Reward Offers. Volume XXIV: THE CASE OF CHERYL RENWICK Paperback – June 3, 2024

19. How To Find All Missing Persons / Unsolved Cases. And Collect All Reward Offers. Volume XXII: THE CASE OF SHARON ELIZABETH FULTON Paperback – June 5, 2024

20. How To Find All Missing Persons / Unsolved Cases. And Collect All Reward Offers. Volume XXII: THE CASE OF SHARON ELIZABETH FULTON Paperback – June 5, 2024

21. How To Find All Missing Persons / Unsolved Cases. And Collect All Reward Offers. Volume XXV: THE CASE OF JANINE VAUGHAN Paperback – June 6, 2024

22. How To Find All Missing Persons / Unsolved Cases. And Collect All Reward Offers. Volume XXVI.: THE CASE OF ROBYN HICKIE Paperback – June 6, 2024

23. How To Find All Missing Persons / Unsolved Cases. And Collect All Reward Offers. Volume XXVII.: THE CASE OF THEO HAYEZ Paperback – June 8, 2024

24. How To Find All Missing Persons / Unsolved Cases. And Collect All Reward Offers. Volume XXX.: THE CASE OF JUANITA NIELSEN Paperback – June 9, 2024

25. How To Find All Missing Persons / Unsolved Cases. And Collect All Reward Offers. Volume XXXIII.: THE CASE OF GORDANA KOTEVSKI Paperback – June 9, 2024

26. How To Find All Missing Persons / Unsolved Cases. And Collect All Reward Offers. Volume XXVIII.: THE CASE OF MELISSA HUNT Paperback – June 8, 2024

27. How To Find All Missing Persons / Unsolved Cases. And Collect All Reward Offers. Volume XXXIV: THE CASE OF MARIA SMITH REAL NAME MARIA STERT Paperback – June 10, 2024

28. How To Find All Missing Persons / Unsolved Cases. And Collect All Reward Offers. Volume XXXX.: THE CASE OF PAULINE SOWRY Paperback – June 16, 2024

29. How To Find All Missing Persons / Unsolved Cases. And Collect All Reward Offers. Volume XXXIX.: THE CASE OF STUART SPEIES WHO SWAPPED WITH TOM PHILLIPS Paperback – June 18, 2024

30. How To Find All Missing Persons / Unsolved Cases. And Collect All Reward Offers. Volume XXXXI.: THE CASE OF JACK O SULLIVAN Paperback – June 18, 2024

31. How To Find All Missing Persons / Unsolved Cases. And Collect All Reward Offers. Volume XXXVIII.: THE CASE OF COLLEEN WALKER-GRAIG [REAL SURNAME STERT] Paperback – June 18, 2024

32. How To Find All Missing Persons / Unsolved Cases. And Collect All Reward Offers. Volume XXXXII.: THE CASE OF CALEB ALYN BROWN Paperback – June 19, 2024

33. How To Find All Missing Persons / Unsolved Cases. And Collect All Reward Offers. Volume XXXXV.: THE CASE OF JOANNE SHEEN-SMITH Paperback – June 20, 2024

34. The Perfect Orphans Laws And Their Rights To Their Own Property.: Extracts From The Book Of Creation Paperback – June 21, 2024

35. How To Find All Missing Persons / Unsolved Cases. And Collect All Reward Offers. Volume L. THE CASE OF ARLENE McLEAN Paperback – June 24, 2024

36. How To Find All Missing Persons / Unsolved Cases. And Collect All Reward Offers. Volume XXXXVII: THE CASE OF AS IT HAPPENS Paperback – June 24, 2024

37. How To Find All Missing Persons / Unsolved Cases. And Collect All Reward Offers. Volume XXXXVI.: THE CASE OF JEVELLE BALMAIN-SMITH Paperback – June 20, 2024

38. How To Find All Missing Persons / Unsolved Cases. And Collect All Reward Offers. Volume XXXXIX. THE CASE OF LESLIE ATN KATERNI ALSO KNOWN AS LESLIE ANNE KATNICK Paperback – June 24, 2024

39. How To Find All Missing Persons / Unsolved Cases. And Collect All Reward Offers. Volume LII. THE CASE OF SHELTON MATHERS SANDERS Paperback – June 25, 2024

40. How To Find All Missing Persons / Unsolved Cases. And Collect All Reward Offers. The Formula. Volume LI. THE CASE OF SHELLEY DENISE CONNORS-THOMPSON: INCLUDES DEATH OF SEKAI SEKERUNGU Paperback – June 25, 2024

41. EMBEZZLED. The Missing Person Reward Scheme Is A Big Scam. In Fact A Police Reward $1million Secret $90000-Per-Account-Round Syndicate: Killing and Stealing Orphans' Houses & Creaming the Community. Paperback – June 27, 2024

42. THE SHELVING OF UNSOLVED CASE IS UNLAWFUL WHEN THE POLICE ARE DELIBERATELY KILLING ORPHANS AND HIDING EVIDENCE THIS WAY.: Extracted from EMBEZZLED Paperback – June 29, 2024

43. How To Find All Missing Persons / Unsolved Cases. And Collect All Reward Offers. The Formula. Volume LIV.: THE CASE OF ANN KIMBERLY MATHEWS McANDREW Paperback – June 29, 2024

44. How To Find All Missing Persons / Unsolved Cases. And Collect All Reward Offers. The Formula. Volume LV.: THE CASE OF TROY COOK Paperback – June 30, 2024

45. How To Find All Missing Persons / Unsolved Cases. And Collect All Reward Offers. The Formula. Volume LXII. THE CASE OF MICHAEL GERALD STEELE ROMNOP Paperback – July 4, 2024

46. How To Find All Missing Persons / Unsolved Cases. And Collect All Reward Offers. The Formula. Volume LVV. THE CASE OF ZACHERY LEFAVE STORN Paperback – July 4, 2024

47. How To Find All Missing Persons / Unsolved Cases. And Collect All Reward Offers. The Formula. Volume LXI. THE CASE OF CARSON MCNUTT Paperback – July 4, 2024

48. How To Find All Missing Persons / Unsolved Cases. And Collect All Reward Offers. The Formula. Volume LVIV. THE CASE OF ALLAN KENLEY MATHESON Paperback – July 4, 2024

49. How To Find All Missing Persons / Unsolved Cases. And Collect All Reward Offers. The Formula. Volume LVIII. THE CASE OF IAN THOMERS MACKEGIAN Paperback – July 4, 2024

50. CRIMESTOPPERS' ROLE IN ABETTING AND AIDING THE POLICE IN THE KILLINGS OF ORPHANS, STEALING OF THEIR HOUSES AND IN THE SHELVING OF CASES IS UNLAWFUL. Paperback – July 4, 2024

51. How To Find All Missing Persons / Unsolved Cases. And Collect All Reward Offers. The Formula. Volume LIII.: THE CASE OF MARGARET ADRENALS AND MICAEL ... ASLO KNOWN AS BARRY SHERMAN AND HONEY SHERMAN Paperback – July 4, 2024

52. How To Find All Missing Persons / Unsolved Cases. And Collect All Reward Offers. The Formula. Volume LXIV. THE CASE OF JAESTER SLATER-JAY KNOWN AS JAY SLATER

53. COURT OF CREATION ON EARTH'S CASE BUNDLE THE SHELVING OF UNSOLVED CASES IS UNLAWFUL WHEN THE POLICE ARE DELIBERATELY KILLING ORPHANS AND HIDING ... NOVA SCOTIA ALL 20 MISSING PERSONS CASES. Paperback – July 8, 2024

54. How To Find All Missing Persons / Unsolved Cases. And Collect All Reward Offers. The Formula. Volume LVI. THE CASE OF JESS MORRISSEY-ROBERTSON JONES Paperback – July 8, 2024

55. COURT OF CREATION ON EARTH'S CASE BUNDLE THE SHELVING OF UNSOLVED CASES IS UNLAWFUL WHEN THE POLICE ARE DELIBERATELY KILLING ORPHANS AND HIDING ... QUEENSLAND 20 MISSING PERSONS CASES. Paperback – July 9, 2024

56. CREDIBLE DEFENSE TO THE ALEC BALDWIN CASE: Credible Evidence To Exonerate Alec Baldwin Paperback – July 15, 2024

57. COURT OF CREATION ON EARTH THE SHELVING OF UNSOLVED CASES IS UNLAWFUL WHEN THE POLICE ARE DELIBERATELY KILLING ORPHANS AND HIDING EVIDENCE THIS WAY.: UNITED STATES OF AMERICA 20 MISSING PERSONS CASES. Paperback – July 9, 2024

58. COURT OF CREATION ON EARTH THE SHELVING OF UNSOLVED CASES IS UNLAWFUL WHEN THE POLICE ARE DELIBERATELY KILLING ORPHANS AND HIDING EVIDENCE THIS WAY.: BRITAIN 20 MISSING PERSONS CASES. Paperback – July 9, 2024

59. How To Find All Missing Persons / Unsolved Cases. And Collect All Reward Offers. Volume LIX. THE CASE OF THE VICTIMS OF POLICE OFFICER ASEROPERS CATERINA Paperback – July 22, 2024

60. How To Find All Missing Persons / Unsolved Cases. And Collect All Reward Offers. Volume LVIII. THE CASE OF MATTHEW PERRY AND EL INE PARK-TSU Paperback – July 22, 2024

61. How To Live Up To 1 Million Years Looking Like When You Were 2 Years Old: hailhailhailodavidgomadza.startx8.initialise.start Paperback – July 24, 2024

62. Introducing Nickel As The New Currency Paperback – July 25, 2024

63. COURT OF CREATION ON EARTH THE SHELVING OF UNSOLVED CASES IS UNLAWFUL WHEN THE POLICE ARE DELIBERATELY KILLING ORPHANS AND HIDING EVIDENCE THIS WAY.: NEW ZEALAND Paperback – July 9, 2024

64. How To Find All Missing Persons / Unsolved Cases And Collect All Reward Offers The Formula. Volume LXX THE CASE OF THE VICTIMS OF POLICE OFFICER AEROSITY AEROSTY Paperback – July 31, 2024

65. How to Find All Missing Persons / Unsolved Cases and Collect All Reward Offers. The Formula. Volume LXXI THE CASE OF ELLE ESTELLE-PARKINSON Paperback – August 3, 2024

66. How To Find All Missing Persons / Unsolved Cases And Collect All Reward Offers The Formula. Volume LXXII. NEW ZEALAND. THE CASE OF THE VICTIMS OF POLICE OFFICER ASEROSTY ASEROSITY Paperback – August 6, 2024

67. How To Find All Missing Persons / Unsolved Cases And Collect All Reward Offers The Formula. Volume LXXIII. NEW ZEALAND & AUSTRALIA THE CASE OF THE VICTIMS OF POLICE OFFICER ATERSER AOTAOA Paperback – August 8, 2024

68. How To Find All Missing Persons / Unsolved Cases And Collect All Reward Offers The Formula. Volume LXXIV. BRITAIN, GERMANY, DUTCH BRAZIL & NEW ... VICTIMS OF POLICE OFFICER ATENOSTY ATENOSITY Paperback – August 9, 2024

69. How to Find All Missing Persons / Unsolved Cases and Collect All Reward Offers the Formula. Volume LXXV. BRITAIN. THE CASE OF THE VICTIMS OF POLICE OFFICER ATENOSTY ATENOSITY: [continued] Paperback – August 10, 2024

70. Earth2 What Can Be of Humans with And Without YAHWEH's Creation and How to Resolve the Issues Raised. A Look at Creation and YAHWEH's Adjustments' Implications on Humans 21 August 2024
71. B] THE SHELVING OF UNSOLVED CASE IS UNLAWFUL WHEN THE POLICE ARE DELIBERATELY KILLING ORPHANS AND HIDING EVIDENCE THIS WAY.
72. C] EMBEZZLED. The Missing Person Reward Scheme Is A Big Scam. In Fact, A Police Reward $1million Secret $90000-Per-Account Round Syndicate.
Killing and Stealing Orphans' Houses & Creaming the Community.
73. D] CRIMESTOPPERS' ROLE IN ABETTING AND AIDING THE POLICE IN THE KILLINGS OF ORPHANS, STEALING OF THEIR HOUSES AND IN THE SHELVING OF CASES IS UNLAWFUL.
74. E] <u>The Perfect Orphans Laws And Their Rights To Their Own Property.: Extracts From The Book Of Creation</u>

F] Credible Evidence to Exonerate Alec Baldwin

I [David Gomadza] rest my case.

www.twofuture.world

I Represent YAHWEH On Earth.

Court of Creation on Earth

I summed up our finding about the whole saga in the book credible evidence to exonerate Alec Baldwin where I argued that all this killing of orphans and stealing their properties is

1. Abuse of Power

2. Harassment & Invasion OF Privacy

3. Illegal Collection of Capital Gains Tax Before Sale of Property

4. Targeting & Killings of Orphans

5. Illegal Spying Using Button Cameras

6. Killing the American Dream

7. Falsifying and Withholding Evidence.
Abuse of power

ABOUT THE AUTHOR

David Gomadza visit www.twofuture.world

www.ingramcontent.com/pod-product-compliance
Lightning Source LLC
Chambersburg PA
CBHW051400250726
48656CB00006B/2194